simple words to love by

susan rutledge

50 ways to keep your relationship fresh & strong

WILLOW
BEND
PRESS

Simple Words to Love By: 50 Ways To Keep Your Relationship Fresh & Strong

Copyright © 2019 by Susan Rutledge. All rights reserved.

No part of this publication may be reproduced, stored in a retrieval system or transmitted, in any form or by any means - electronic, mechanical, photocopying, recording or otherwise, without prior written permission from the publisher, except for the inclusion of brief quotations in a review.

Published by Willow Bend Press, Prosper, TX

willowbendpress.com

Hardback ISBN-13: 978-1-950019-01-4

Paperback ISBN-13: 978-1-950019-03-8

First Printing, February 2019

Author: Susan Rutledge

www.susanrutledge.com

Publisher's Cataloging-in-Publication Data

Names: Rutledge, Susan, author.

Title: Simple words to love by: 50 ways to keep your relationship fresh & strong / Susan Rutledge.

Description: Prosper, TX: Willow Bend Press, 2019.

Identifiers: ISBN 978-1-950019-01-4 (Hardcover) | 978-1-950019-03-8 (pbk.)

Subjects: LCSH Love. | Marriage. | Romance. | BISAC FAMILY & RELATIONSHIPS /Love & Romance | FAMILY & RELATIONSHIPS /Marriage & Long-Term Relationships

Classification: LCC BF575.L8 .R879 2019 | DDC 306.7--dc23

for grant

forgive
and let it go

initiate

romance

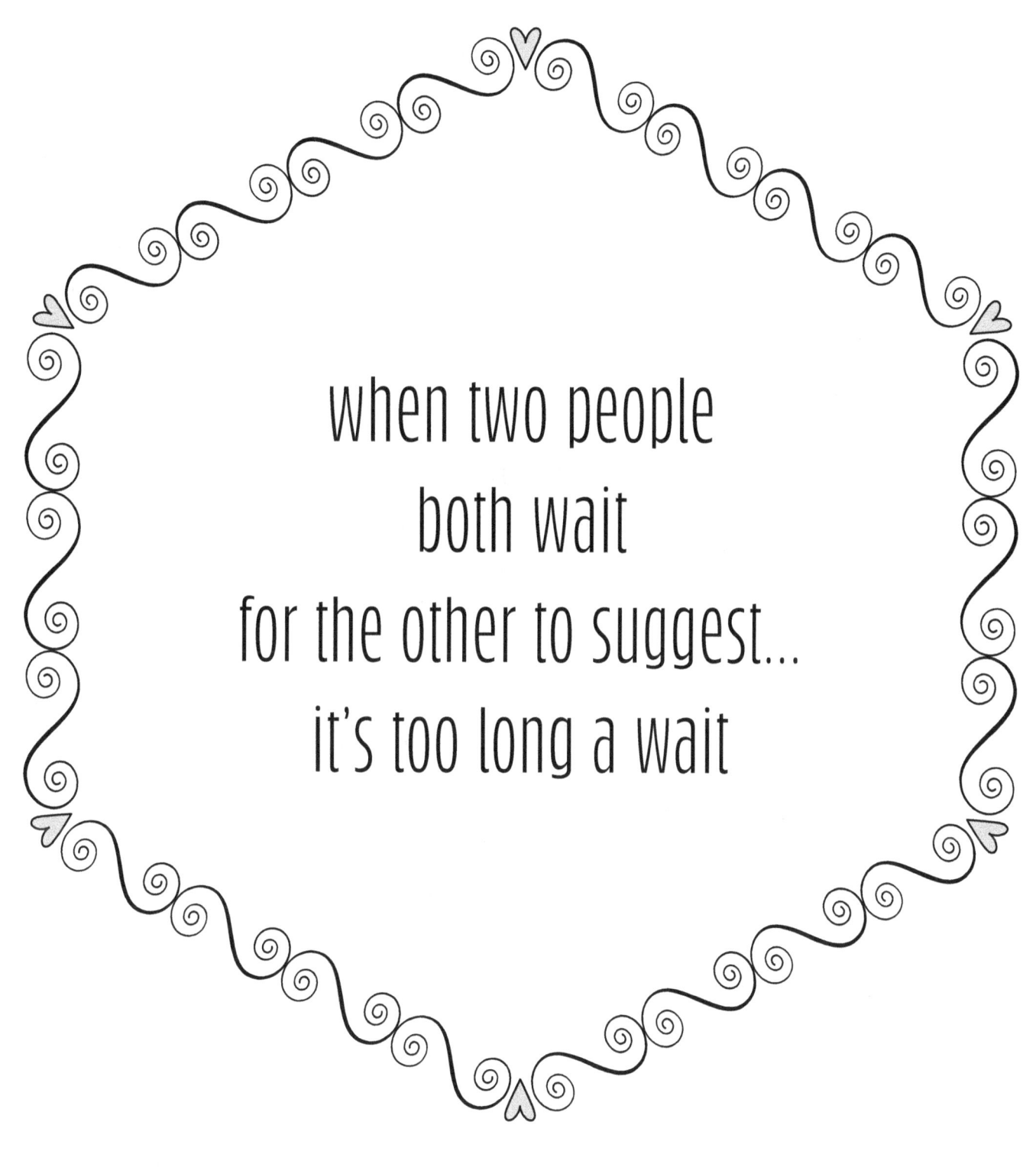

when two people
both wait
for the other to suggest...
it's too long a wait

remember
the good things

good always triumphs
over bad;
love wins when you
hold on to the good

laugh
and have fun

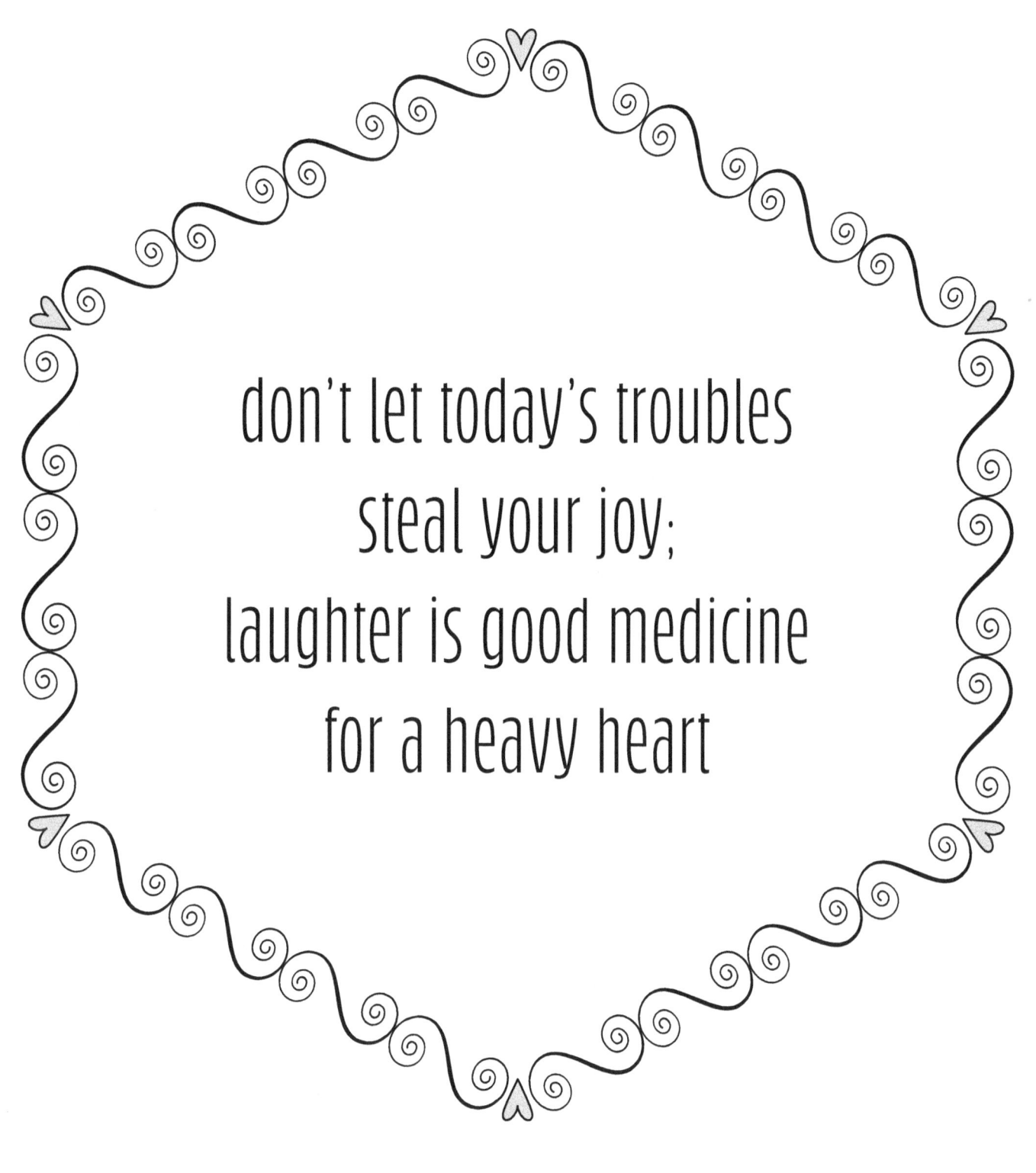

give
without expectation

listen

with undivided attention

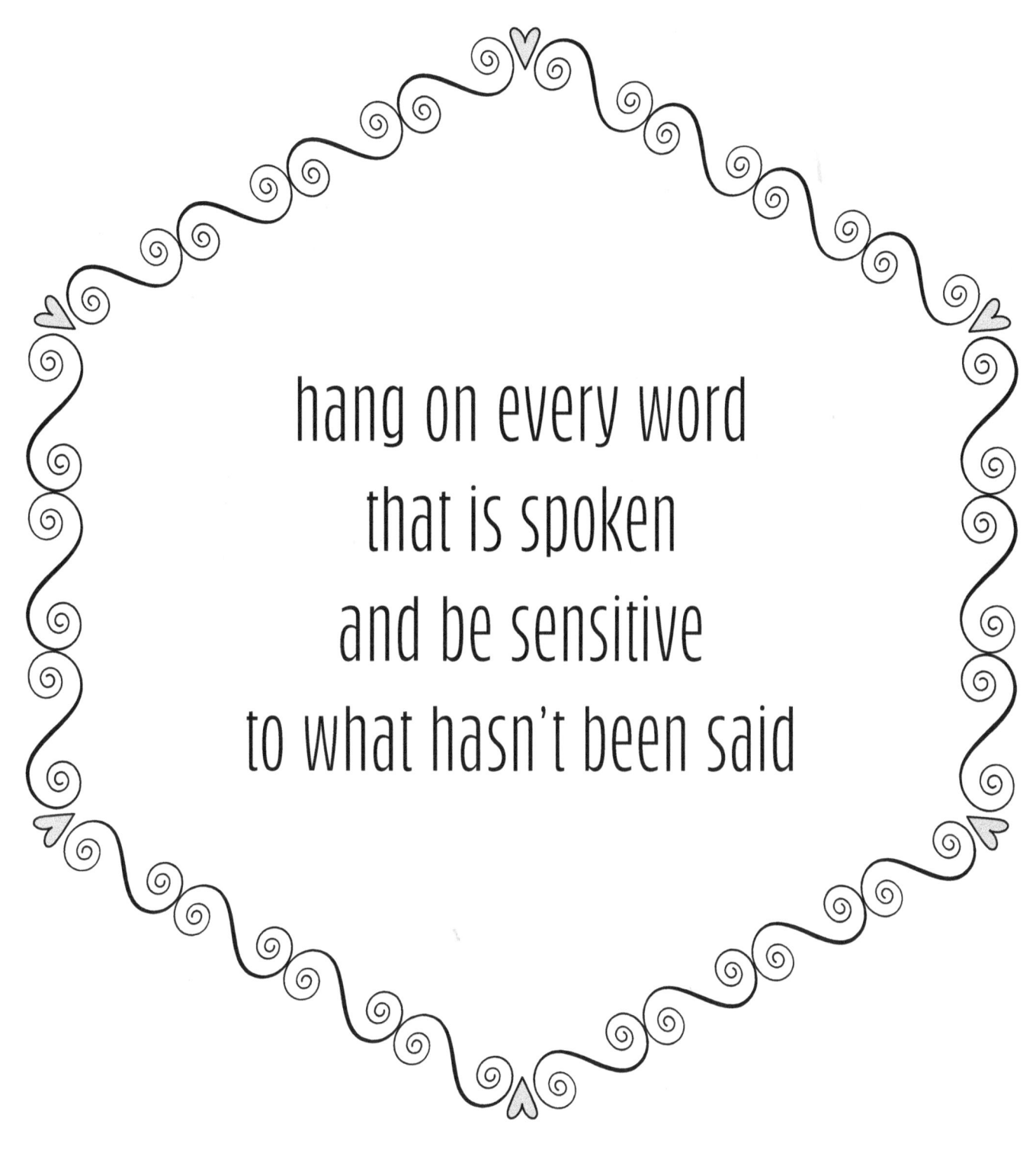
hang on every word
that is spoken
and be sensitive
to what hasn't been said

make love

like there is no tomorrow

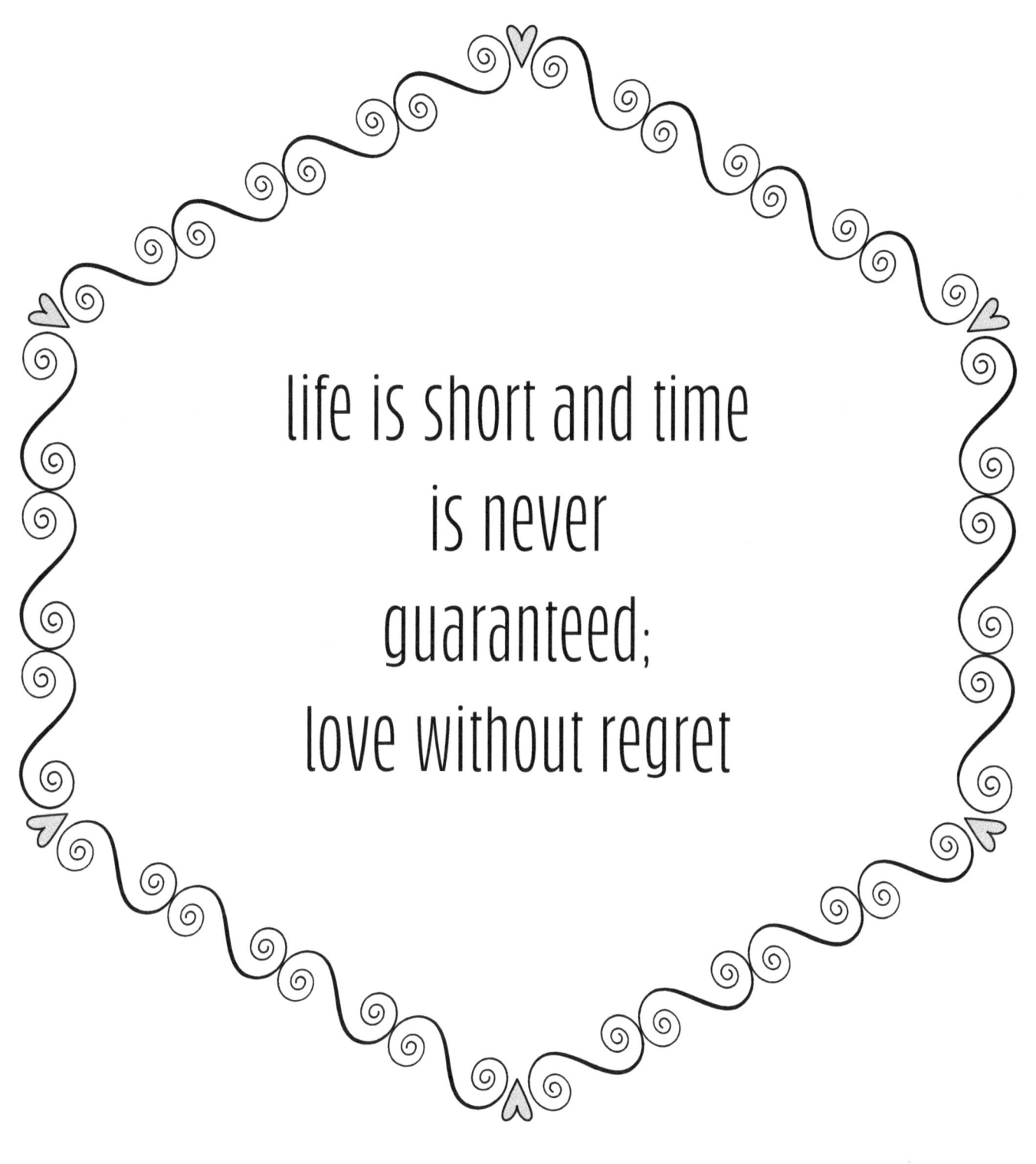

life is short and time is never guaranteed; love without regret

always
be honest

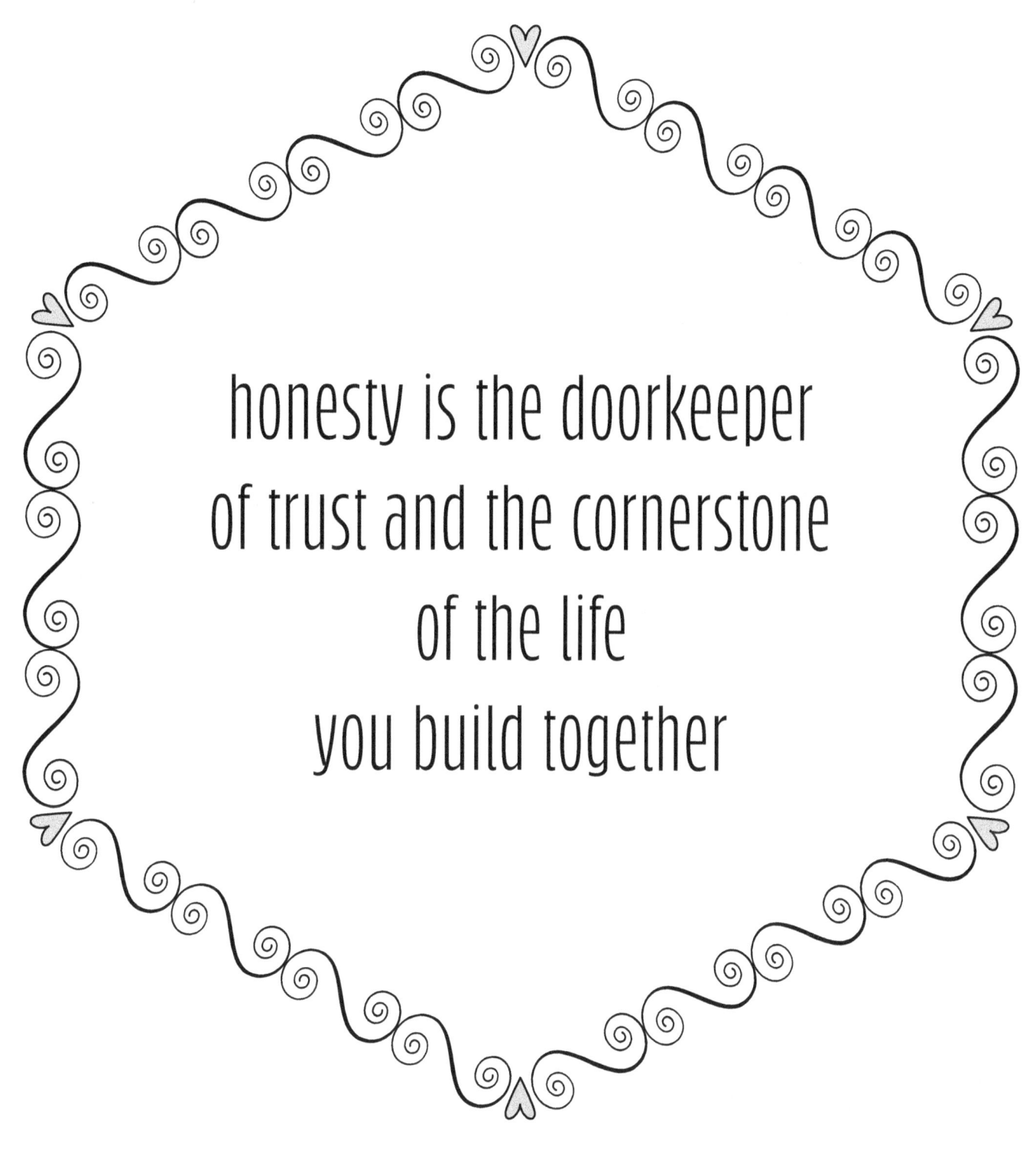
honesty is the doorkeeper of trust and the cornerstone of the life you build together

pick up

after yourself

play
for keeps

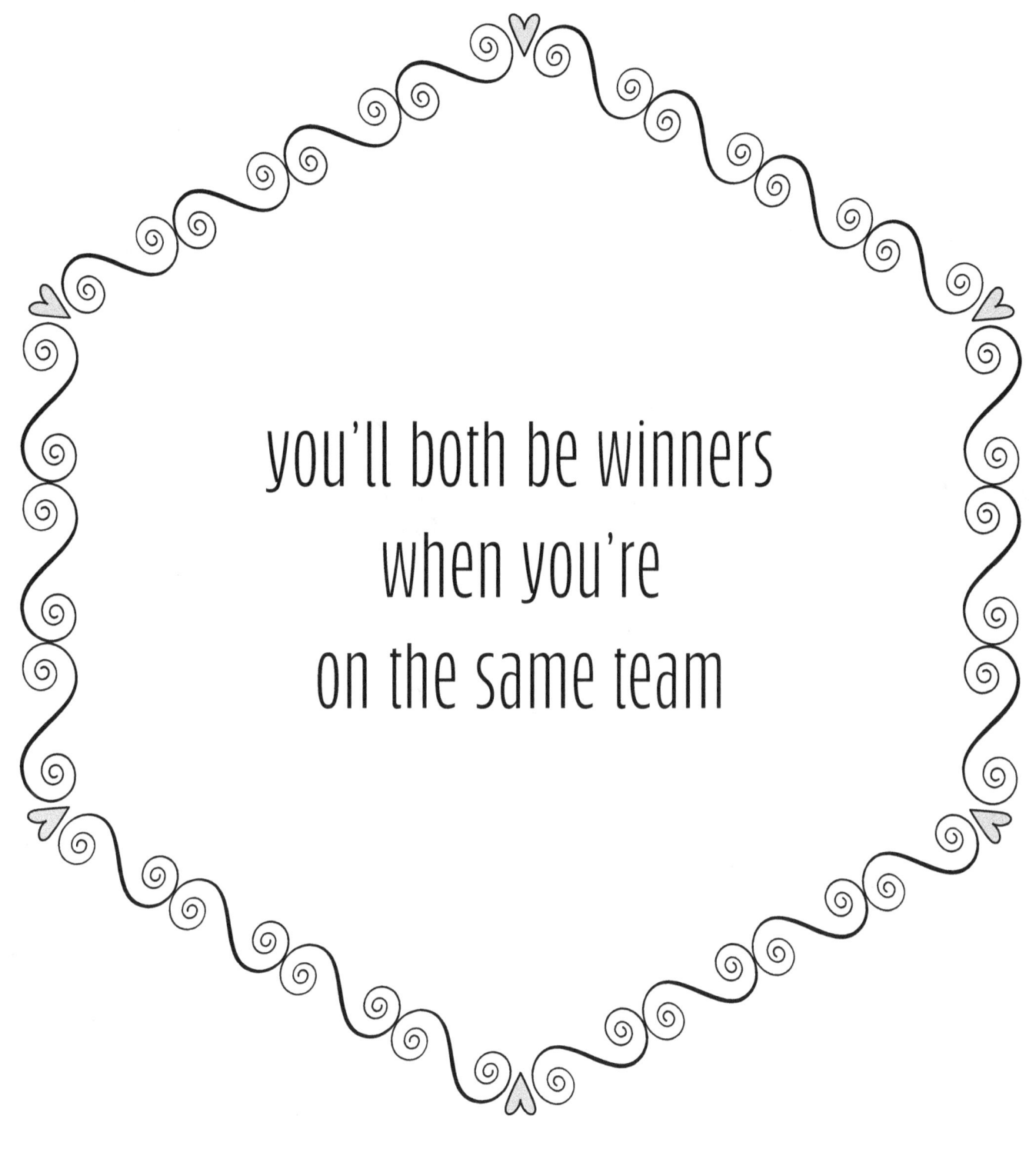
you'll both be winners when you're on the same team

practice
contentment

seek fulfillment
in the grass
on *your* side
of the fence

hurry

home

establish

traditions

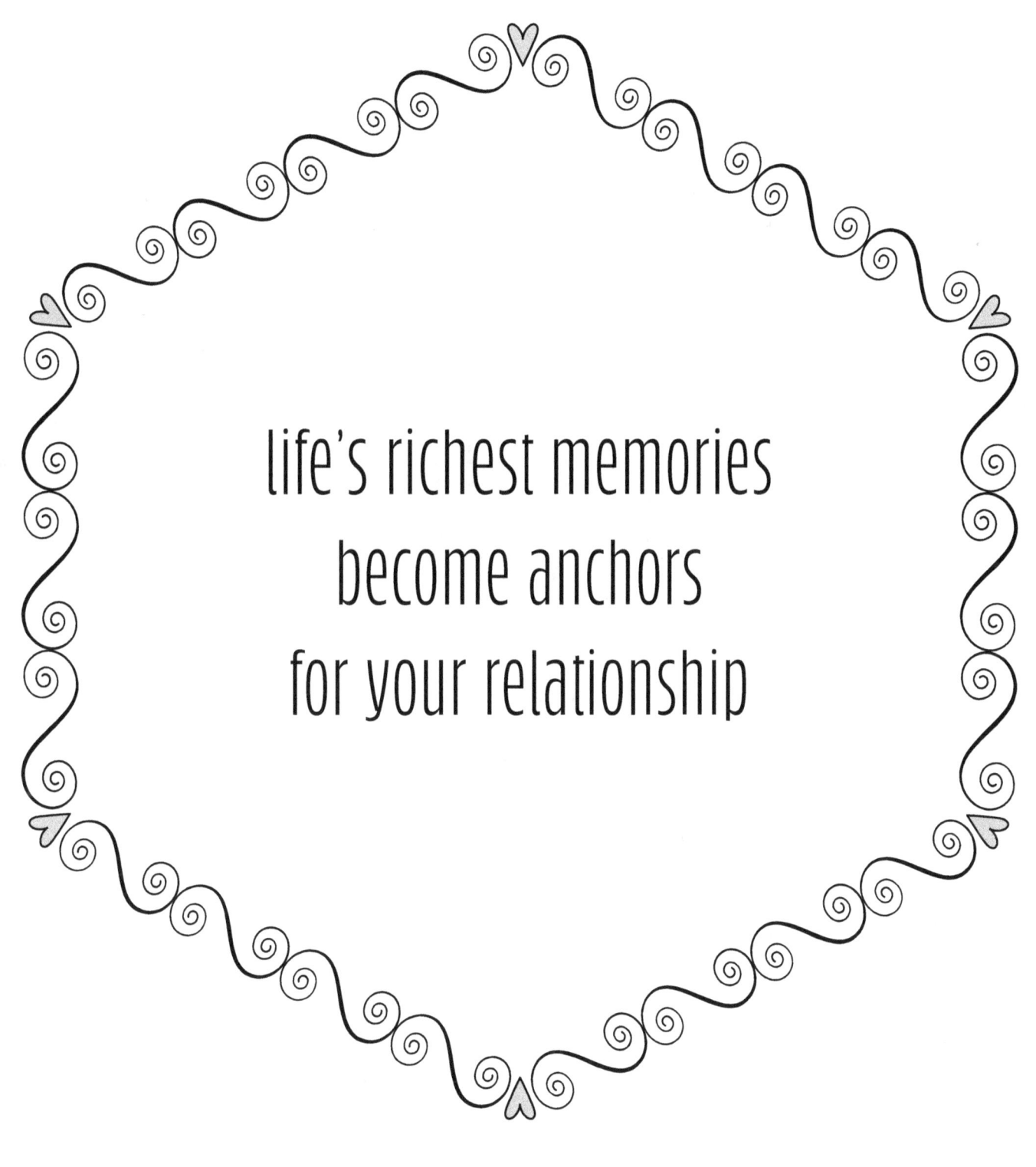
life's richest memories become anchors for your relationship

dive
deep

don't tiptoe
through shallow waters;
immerse yourselves
in one another

never

give up

touch
often

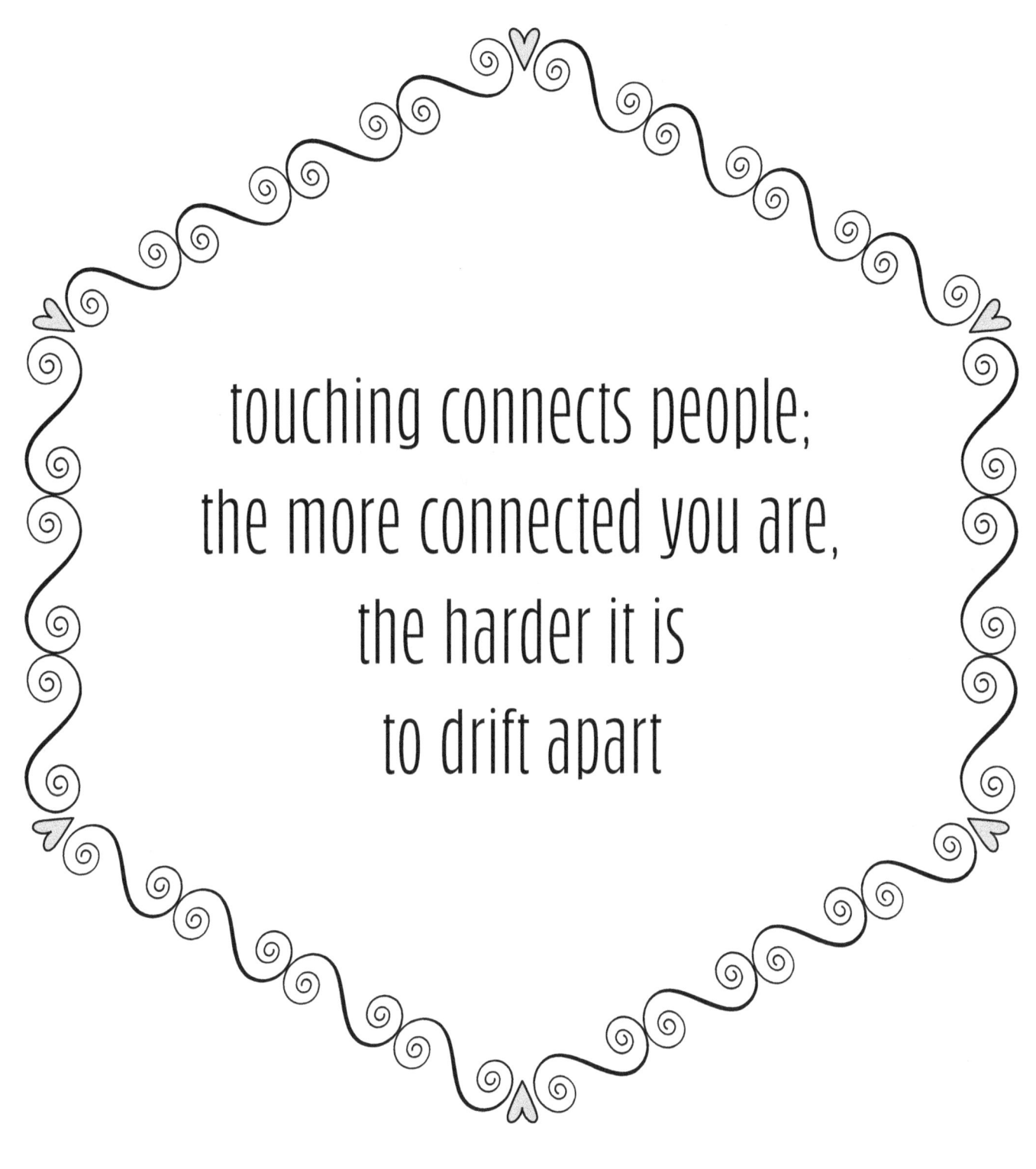

touching connects people;
the more connected you are,
the harder it is
to drift apart

live
a love story

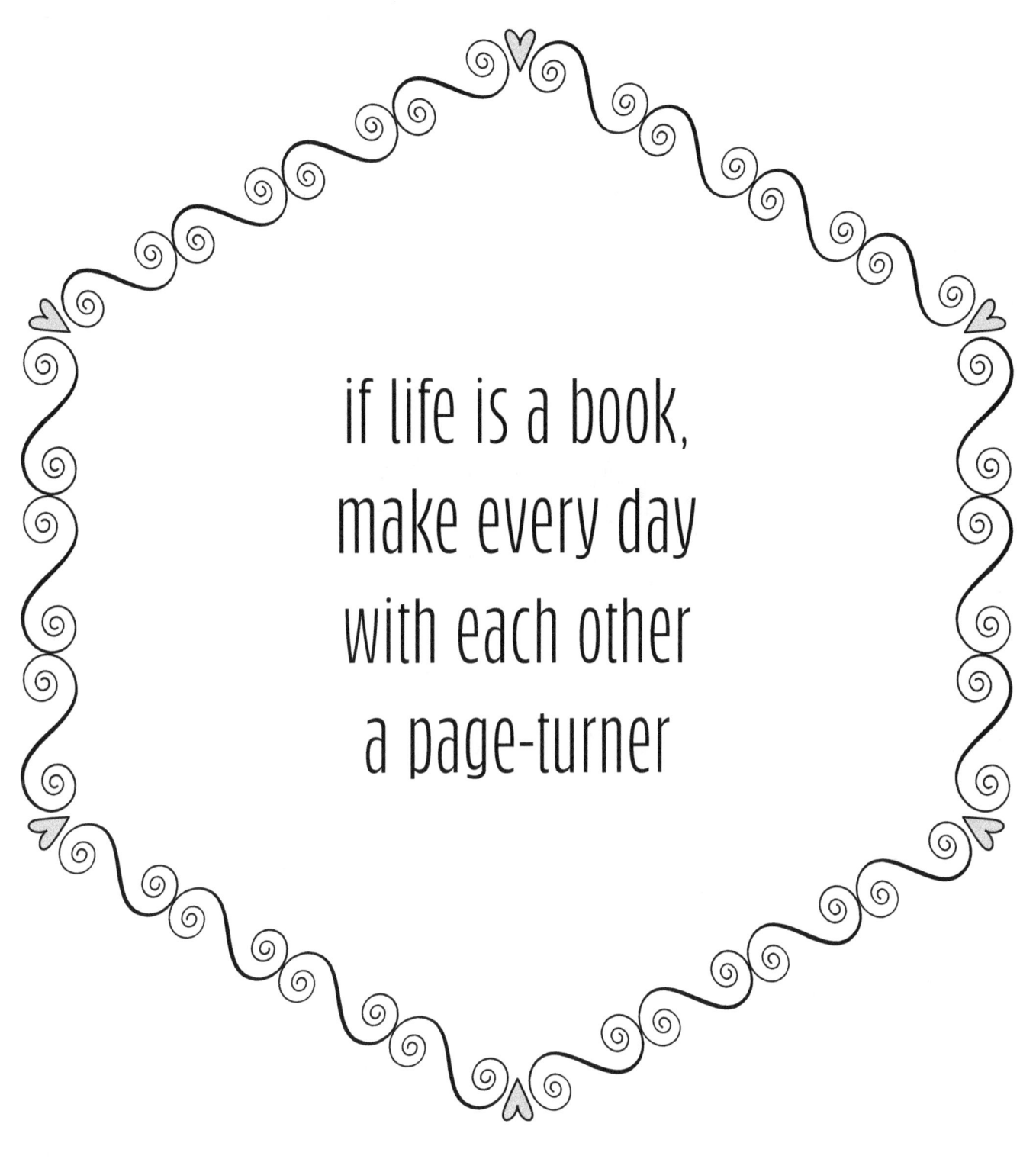

if life is a book, make every day with each other a page-turner

agree
to disagree

run
to each other

through every high
and every low,
seek praise and comfort
at home

keep
talking

surprise
and excite

explore
creation

broaden your
shared experiences
and deepen your sense
of adventure

discuss

problems

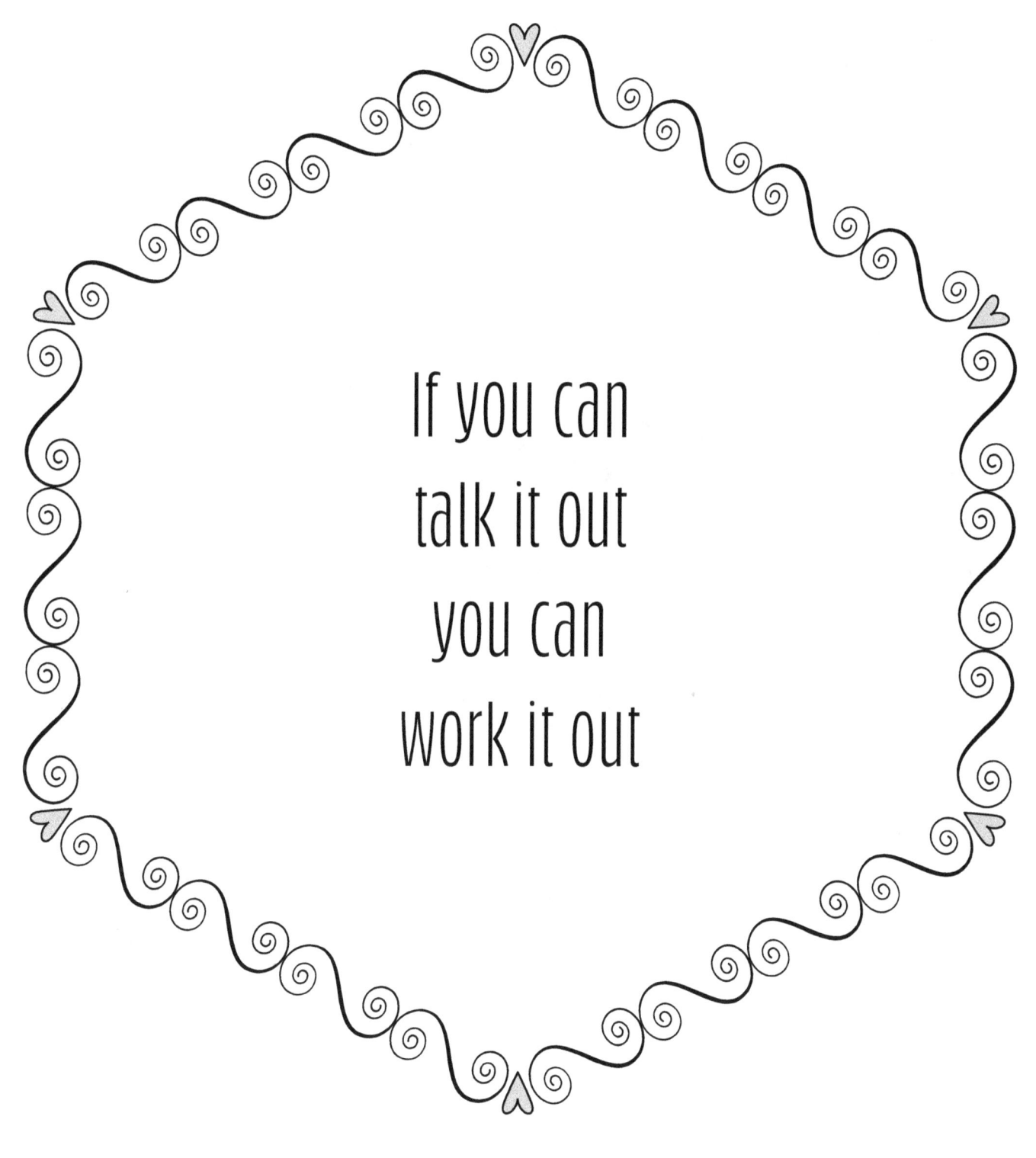

invest

in the future

put one another first today and every day

spoil
your lover

nothing is ever too much
when it comes
to giving
love

express

gratitude

cherish

every moment

when the sun goes to bed,
another day slips away forever;
make the most of today
and the love you share

allow
for differences

crush

temptation

whisper

"I love you"

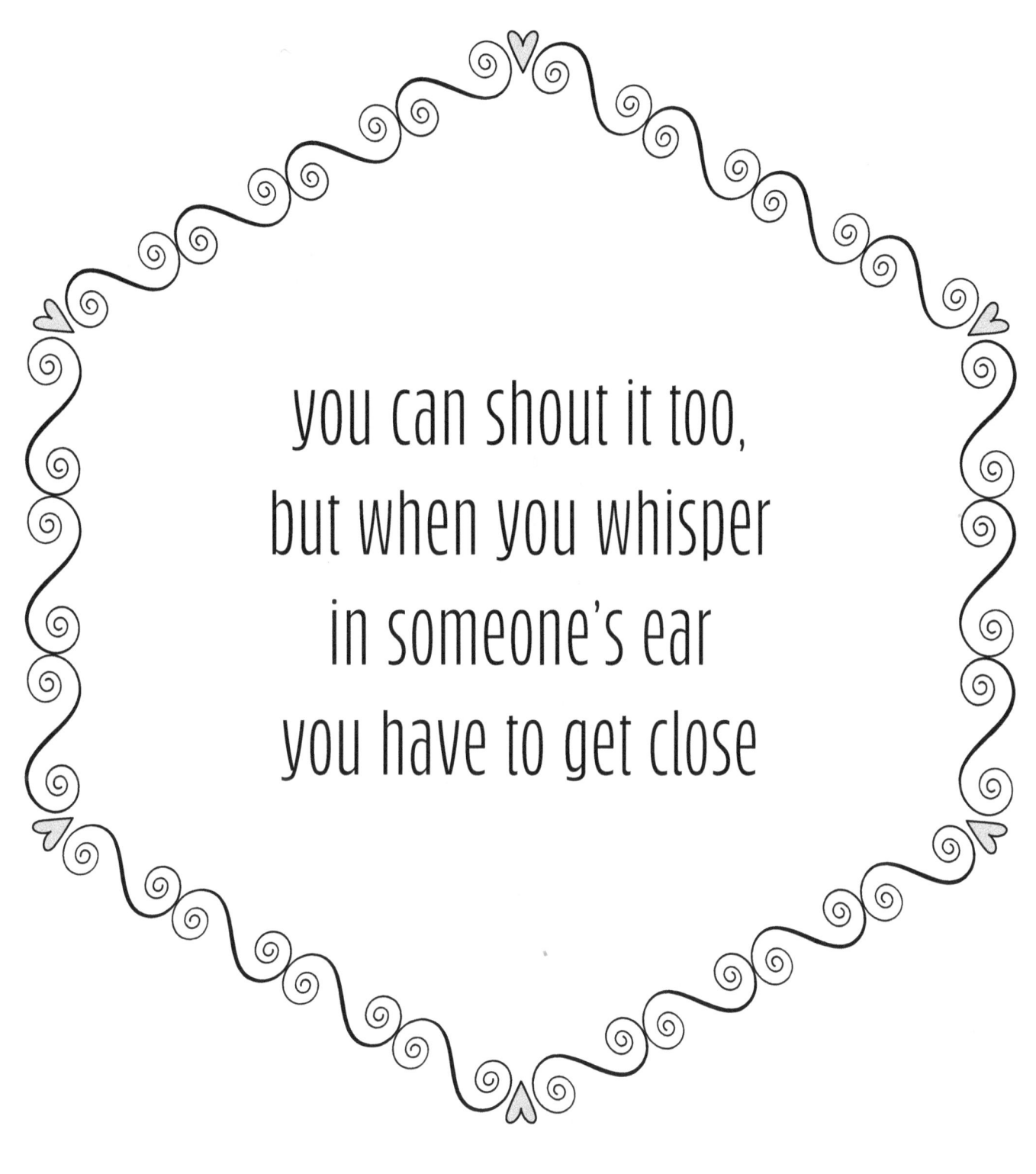

you can shout it too,
but when you whisper
in someone's ear
you have to get close

go

together

the bad
will be easier
and the good
will be better

guard
your time

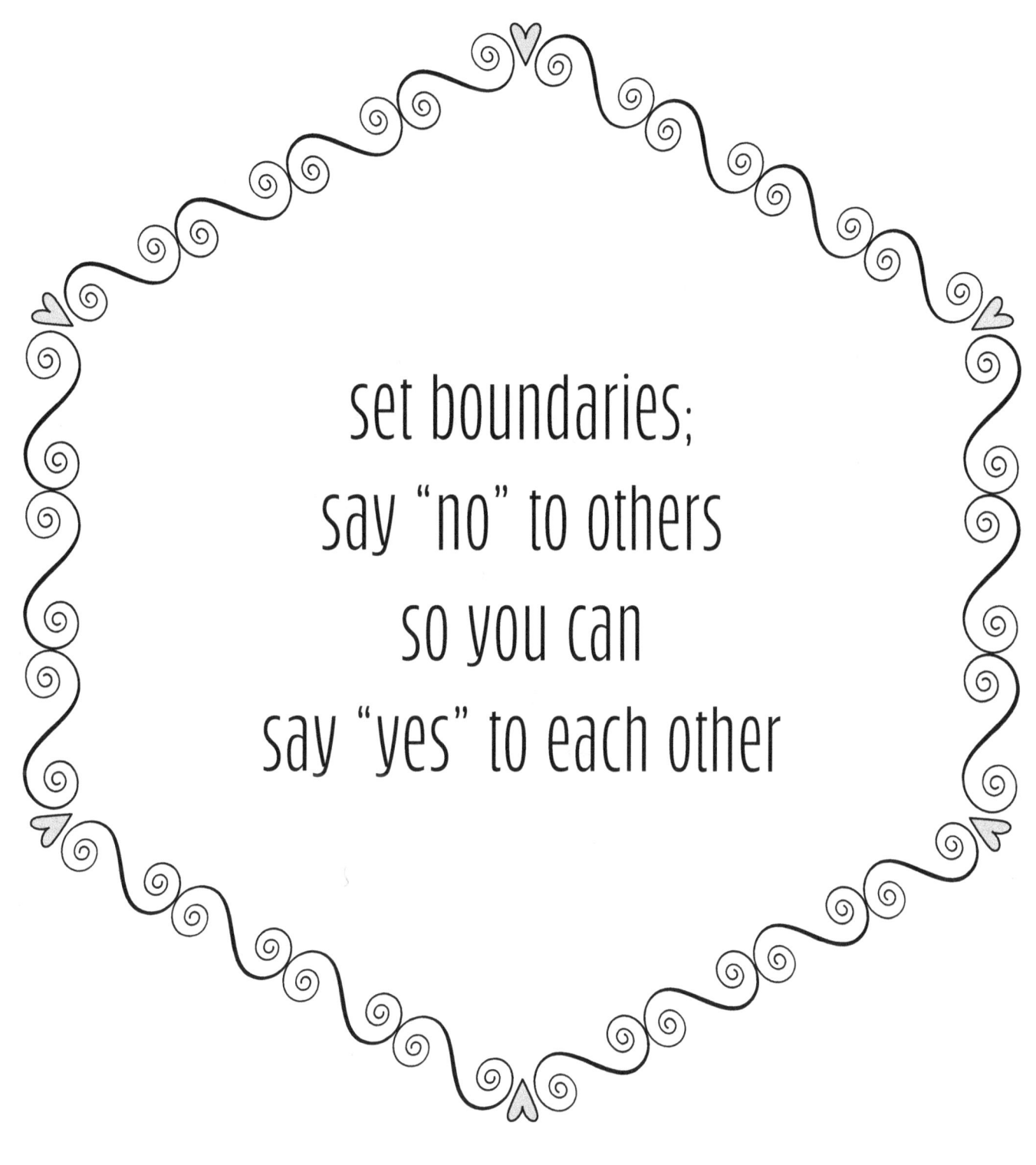

respond

in love

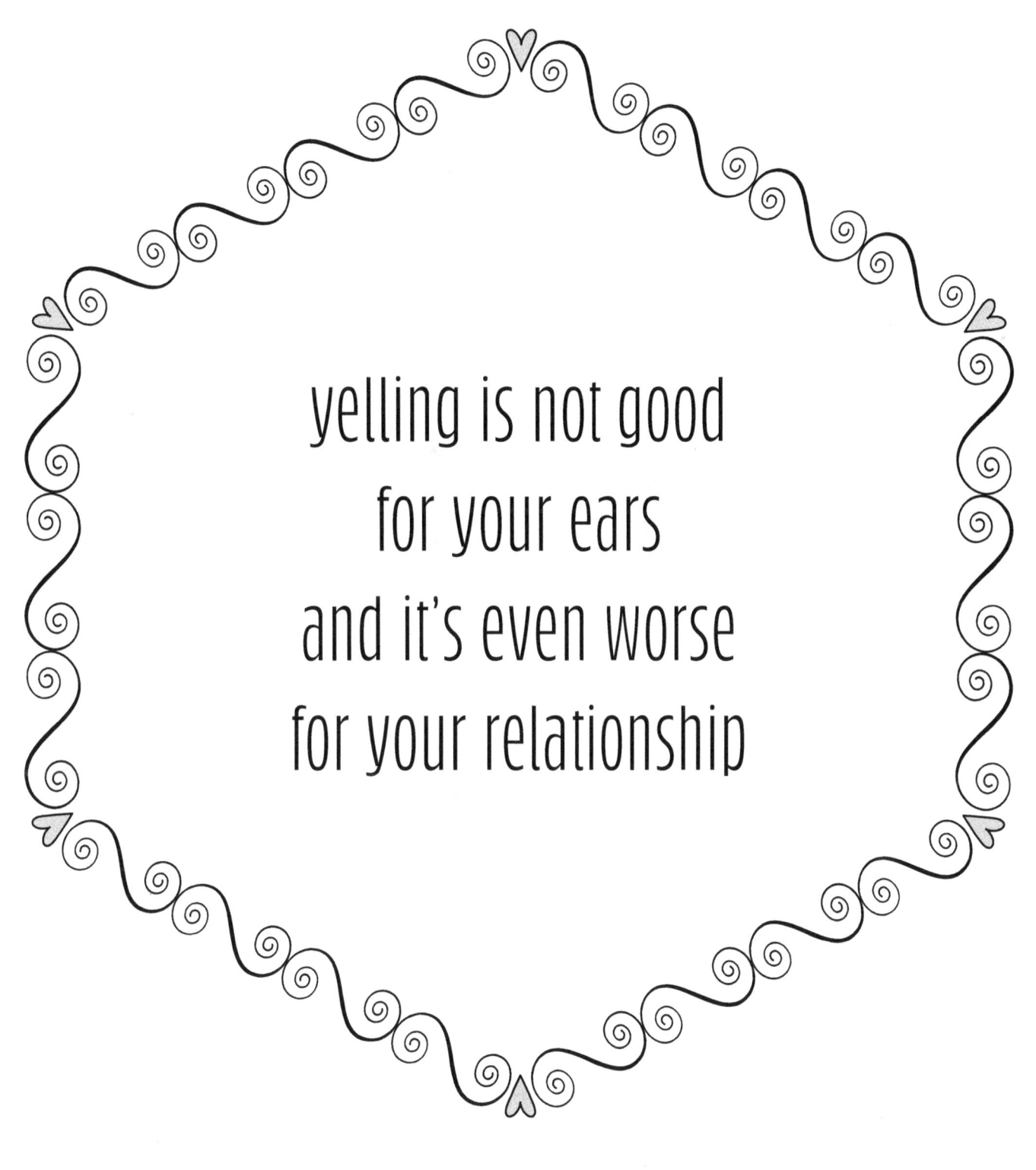

plan
a "demo" day

tear down
any walls
that hide who you are
from the one you love

slow dance

anywhere

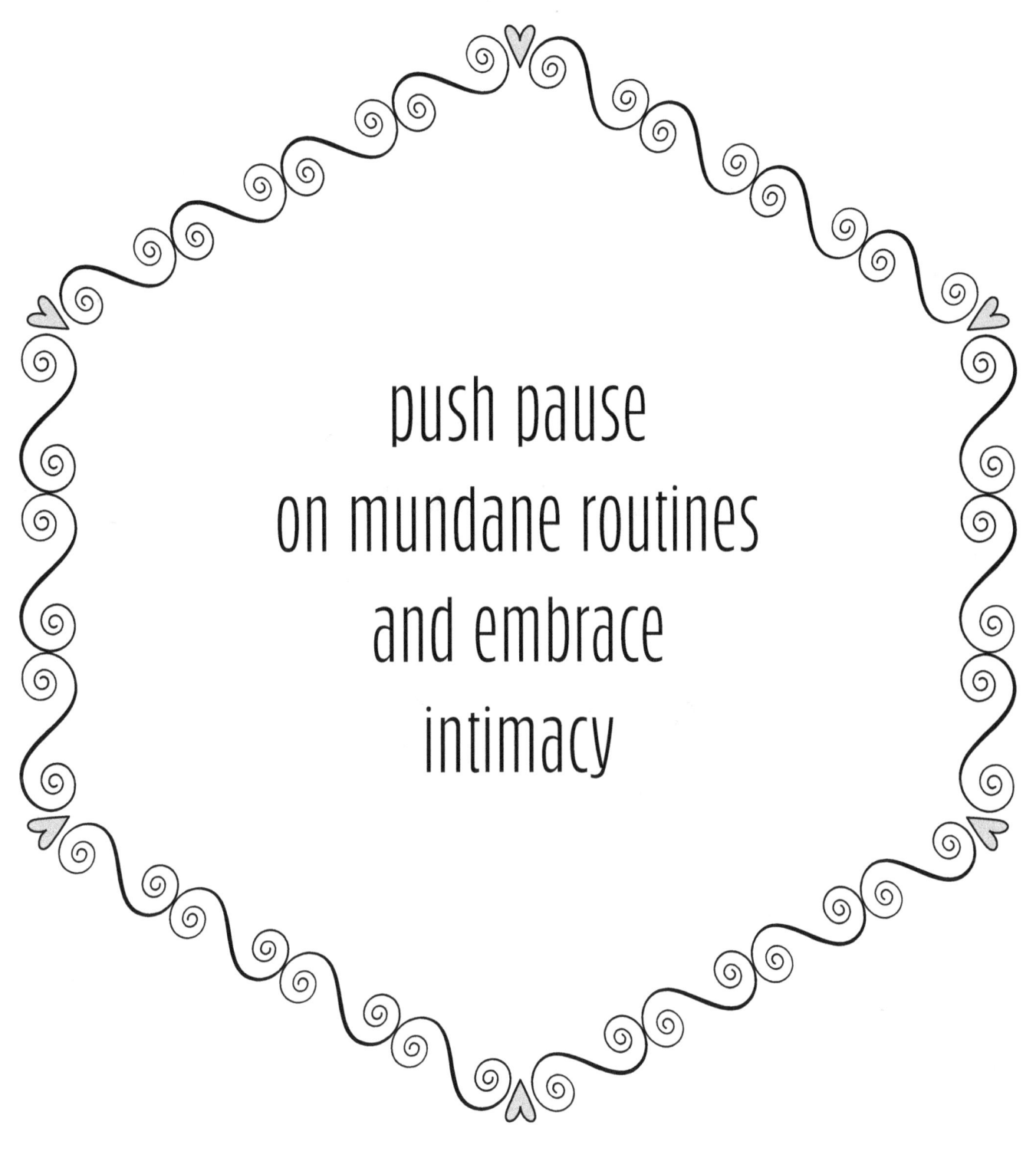
push pause
on mundane routines
and embrace
intimacy

take
the high road

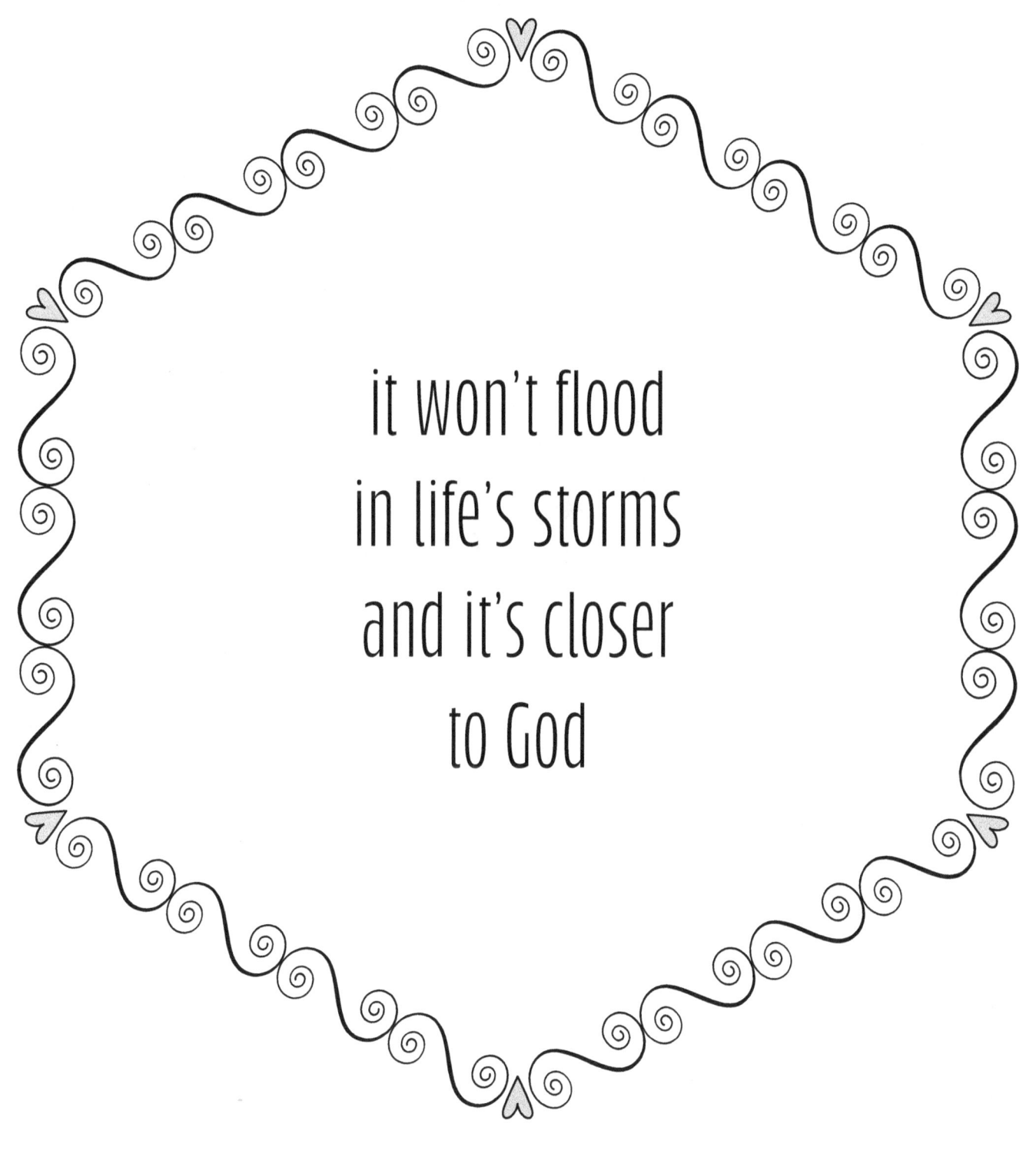

it won't flood
in life's storms
and it's closer
to God

stop
and smell the roses

make time to
enjoy and appreciate
the beauty of life
and your love

abandon
anything that keeps you apart

put aside distractions and be one another's greatest attraction

speak
kindly

honor

promises

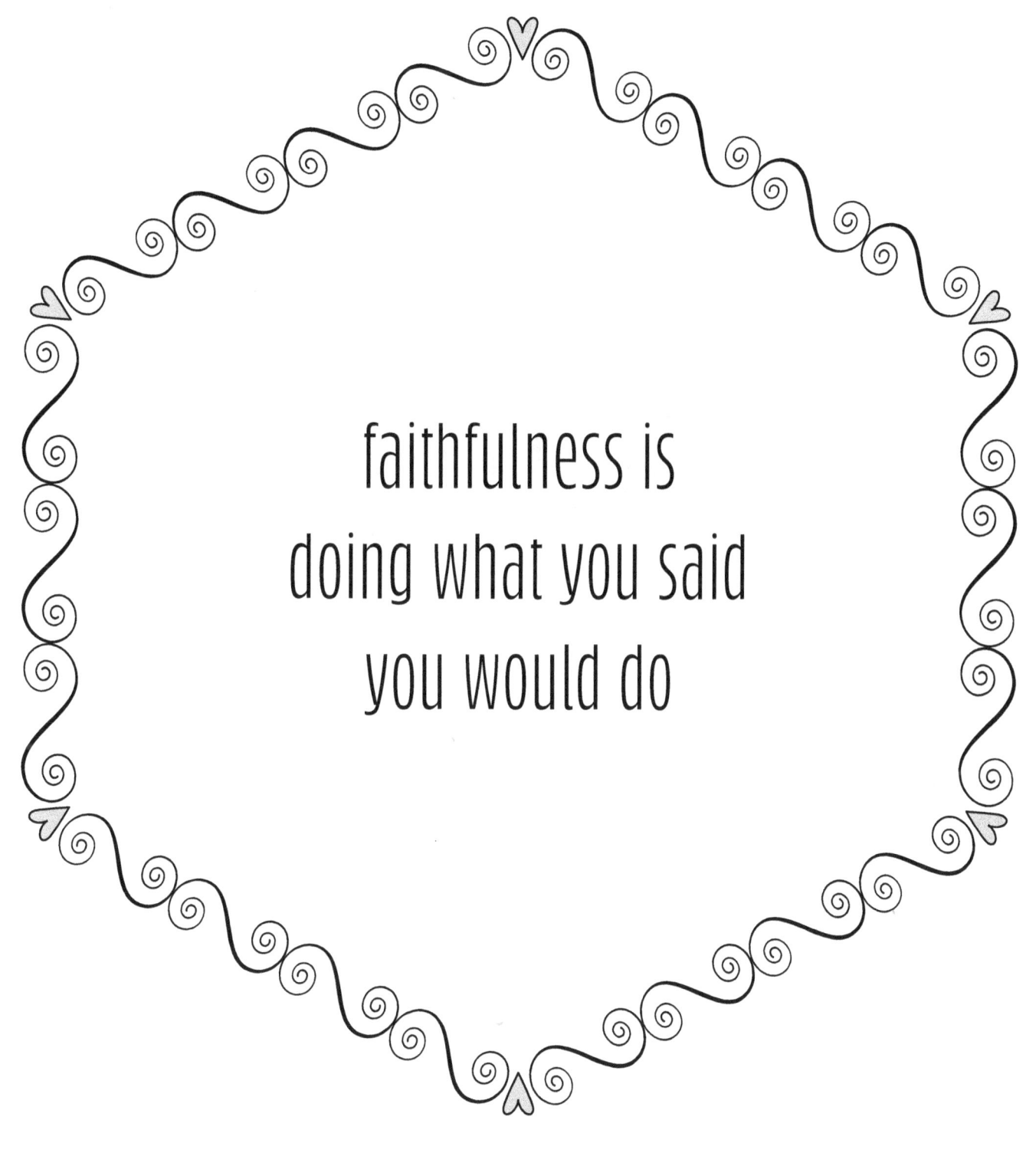

faithfulness is
doing what you said
you would do

think
positive

it's more enjoyable
to spend time
with someone whose
glass is half full

protect
the other person's feelings

harsh words cannot
be unsaid;
guard your tongue and
never speak in anger

fight
to keep passion alive

no fire
burns forever
without someone
tending to it

apologize
first

you can always find
a good reason
to be the first one
to say, "I'm sorry"

love
unconditionally

serve

joyfully

give yourself
wholeheartedly,
doing all you can do
for one another

support
each other's dreams

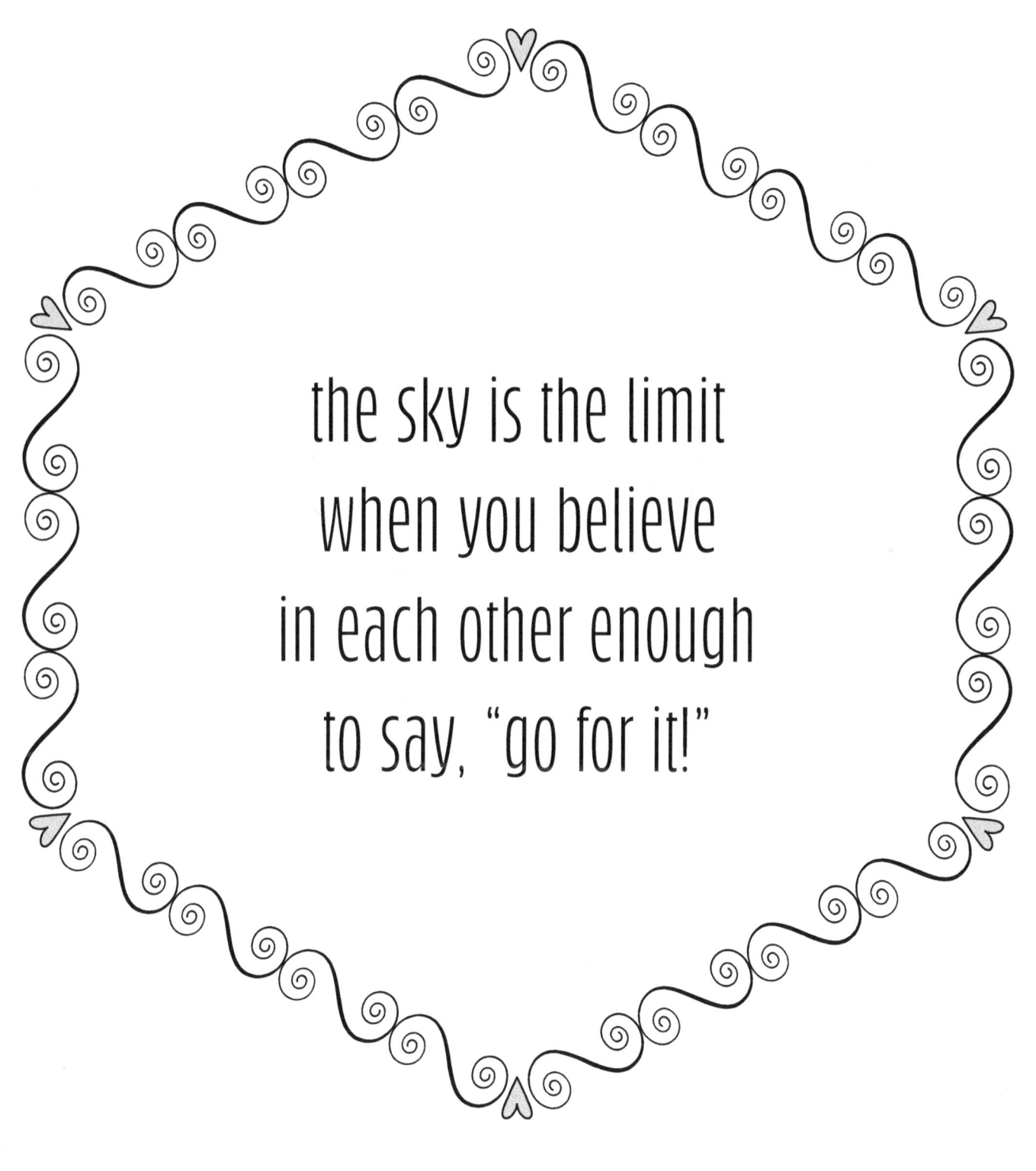

the sky is the limit
when you believe
in each other enough
to say, "go for it!"

celebrate

the little things

pray
together

just be

sometimes that's enough

www.ingramcontent.com/pod-product-compliance
Lightning Source LLC
Chambersburg PA
CBHW081201020426
42333CB00020B/2588